An Empty Stage

A COLLECTION OF MONOLOGUES

EDITED BY JK LARKIN

An Empty Stage – A Collection of Monologues

Copyright © 2023 by JK Larkin

All rights reserved

Published by Red Penguin Books

Bellerose Village, New York

No part of this book may be reproduced in any form or by any electronic or mechanical means, including information storage and retrieval systems, without written permission from the author, except for the use of brief quotations in a book review.

CONTENTS

UNSPOKEN — 1
Rebekah Soumakis

ALICE — 5
Alaina Messineo

BELOVED HUSBAND — 9
Paula Gail Benson

I BELIEVE IN A WORLD OF POSSIBILITIES — 13
David Lange

CLOUDED — 17
Amanda Montoni

LOBSTER OF MY LIFE — 19
An excerpt from the one-act radio play, "Boiled Breakup"
Amanda Montoni

PUNXSUTAWNEY PHIL IS SICK OF THIS SHIT: A MONOLOGUE FOR A PISSED-OFF DEITY — 21
Hayley St. James

I WAS A BOND GIRL — 25
Anita Haas

THE FOOL ON THE HILL — 33
William John Rostron

SMART — 37
A monologue from the play "Standard."
Sage Holloway

SO THIS IS RECOVERY? — 39
A monologue from the play "ED"
Sage Holloway

FRUIT FLIES — 41
Annabel Webster

THE LADY WHO DARED TO GO APE — 45
Nancy Brewka-Clark

YOU CAN'T DO ANYTHING WITHOUT ME — 49
Christina Hoag

PAPER BIRD 57
From the screenplay "Imposter"
Shevaun Cavanaugh Kastl

THE NON-DATE 61
From the Screenplay "Resurrecting Rapunzel"
Shevaun Cavanaugh Kastl

THE PERFECT PURPLE CAPE 65
Gavin Duering

MECONIUM ASPIRATIONS: A PLAY IN TEN
BREATHS 67
Mark Blickley

THE UNSAID OR THE SUPPRESSION 71
Kerri M. Hoffman

YOUR CALL HAS BEEN FORWARDED. 75
Shelbi Cornelison

KILLING TWO BIRDS WITH ONE STONE 79
Shelbi Cornelison

A PEACH AND A TREE 85
Lee Daniel

About the Editor 91
Also From The Red Penguin Collection 93

UNSPOKEN

REBEKAH SOUMAKIS

(*Scene opens on a quiet, dim sideroom. An unnamed speaker is sitting alone, holding still, hand absently grasping the corner of a curtain, and looking attentive, though with unfocused eyes, to the point of being transfixed. A light shines across the speaker, imitating a door opening, accompanied by a creaking sound and, though it dims slightly, the light becomes a sort of spotlight on the speaker. The speaker snaps their attention toward the audience with a look of shock, then relaxes, head shaking, with a wry smile.*) Admit it. You had a feeling you'd find me up here, didn't you? Now, don't look so disappointed. If you ask me, this is the place to be, not the dance hall. Just look around. (*In awe. Holds out hand in a sweeping motion to the small, unimpressive room.*) These walls are as close as an embrace. And these curtains, the way they bunch up in the corners, fanning out here and there, aren't they like blankets? Wrapping around all womblike and warm. And look, they create such incredible shadows! Each one its own set of mazes, dark as the areas in the back of your mind where you keep memories too precious to speak aloud…What? No, I don't think 'cramped' is a more fitting term. (*Pensive, holding out cupped hands and moving them up and down, as if weighing something on a scale.*) 'Dark', yes, but not 'creepy'. You can have 'dark' without 'creepy', you know. (*Shrugs.*) Ah, well, we can agree to disagree. But there's another reason I come here. Listen! Do you hear those notes? Quiet down, just for a moment. Sometimes you feel them more than you hear them. (*Looks off, expectant. Then turns to the audience with slight exasperation, head shaking.*) Not quite the same way as when you crank the bass. You do feel that deep in your chest, but not like this. (*Music begins to play, unmistakably an Asian classical instrument, in somber, understated, peaceful plucking. Speaker barely moves, but the expression and inclination of the body shifts, as if a light from within is dawning across the speaker's face.*) There it is. You hear it now? It's called a guqin. (*Tone changes from quiet excitement to spellbound reverence.*) The sound this instrument makes has rung through the hallways of palaces, serene landscapes, and the cloistered studies of great scholars for over 3,000 years. The ancient Chinese believed it was created by the gods and given to people to enrich their minds and elevate their hearts. Supposedly, it takes a lifetime to master. To get the full experience, ancient scholars had their students master the four arts, music, calligraphy, painting, and a strategy game like chess called 'go' in order to really understand and excel at playing it. But even more goes into it. The guqin itself embodies the philosophy of ancient Chinese thought, including elements of Taoism and Buddhism, like returning to nature, action through inaction...basically, in modern terms, quietly being in the moment rather than using loud, forceful means to prove your value. Or that's my paraphrase, anyway. That's one of my favorite things about the guqin. I've heard that people who judge guqin playing grade students on their understanding of philosophies embodied by the instrument more than their actual playing. Yeah, I was surprised too, but when you think about it, it makes sense. They say understanding of the ancients leads to better knowing the instrument, and therefore, better playing. (*Tone takes on a gravity. Body language and expressions become more grounded as the speaker has a realization.*) And I guess that's why I love it. It's not just an instrument to be played. It's not just a sound to take in. It's not what you do with it. (*Dry laugh.*) If anything, you want to sit still when you hear it, not get up and do things, like dance. (*Shakes head. Then, with growing passion.*) It's what it is. What it means. It embodies a people, a way of thought, of being. It connects to old ways that would otherwise be lost. In fact, people started to lose interest in the guqin with the arrival of a fast-paced modern world, rushing in with the cultural revolution. (*Speaker's posture and expression wilt, as if dying with the guqin itself.*) A way of being almost died with it. But when I hear it play, I know all is not lost. (*Looking up, as if coming back to life again while sharing this realization.*) In a world of movement, of noise, confusion and change, there is a quiet place where stillness is an art to be mastered, silence is still golden, and the ancients continue to speak. (*Shakes self, head snaps back to audience, as if coming out of a trance.*) But I'm sorry, you wanted to bring me back. It's like a club over there, right? The DJ's really cranking it and the dancers are ready to burn up the dance floor? If you say so. Look, I know you really want to go but...you want to stay? (*Surprised.*) Oh. Well...of course you can stay. If it's not too cramped or creepy for you. Thank you. (*With a growing smile.*) Yeah, just slide in next to me.

Rebekah Soumakis is a Children's Librarian who has always loved creative writing and the quiet places where she can cultivate ideas and put them on paper. It was her love of quiet creativity that inspired her to write "Unspoken". Here's hoping that readers will be inspired to appreciate all things understated, intellectual, and quirky. Though this is Rebekah's first monologue, it is also her second piece of published work. The first piece was a poem entitled "Cherry Trees" in Red Penguin's poetry anthology "The Flower Shop on the Corner".

ALICE

ALAINA MESSINEO

On the phone.

SADIE

Right, but she was saying that we both can't be Disney fans because then it's like a Disney household. Like we can't post stuff if we go to or get married there, which I would– (never)

I'm not.

I'm not.

I thought you liked

What's wrong with liking amusement parks?

No, okay,

Why when people hear I like Disney and assume I am a crazy Disney adult

because

A.) maybe I am

I mean I like Disney and I am partially crazy and I am an adult, kind of, I guess now so, And

B.) why, are you mad?

Are you?

Are you mad?

You can say you're mad.

And finally

C.) Disney owns everything and anything so your point is pretty much invalid.

Most of the time they are people who watch football and let me tell you if you are an avid football addict which is watching people chase after a ball with some car and chip commercials thrown in while capitalism royally fucks everyone involved over pretty much which I guess

Disney does too but at least people are happy at Disney not drunk okay a lot are drunk and happy if you are drinking at Disney which ya is fun I guess okay I think I have lost my Wait no

I was going to

Yes I was getting there

Yes

But

Give me like two minutes

Okay

Two minutes

Alice

Hear me out

Disney hates Alice

they do

ALICE

I think Disney hates Alice and they are equally ashamed of Alice and how the story glorifies drugs and all that.

They don't even have a meet and greet station for her or anything she just roams around with random wonderland characters and it's really hard to find her you like cannot even find her because they do not want you to find her because they hate her

You can even find the mad hatter better than her

hell

I had an easier time finding Geppetto

Fucking Geppetto

Who the hell wants to see him

Okay, I guess that was mean, I am sorry Geppetto, but do you see my point? The People want Alice.

A beat.

I swear only straight people watch football

I'd rather go on an Alice scavenger hunt than watch grass die for 3 hours on a shitty flatscreen.

Alaina Messineo (she/her) is an NYC-based Poet, Playwright, Lyricist, Director, and Dramaturg, originally from Rochester New York. Currently, she is a Senior at Marymount Manhattan College with a double concentration in Writing for the Stage and Directing. Her new play Water Doesn't Kill was recently directed by Craig Baldwin this past January. Other playwriting credits include Water Does The Royal Garden (Lucky Rat), Banana Bread Tastes Better When It's Ripe (Obvious Child) (Quarantine Bakeoff), RIGHTS LEFT (Constitution Project) and The Wheel

ALAINA MESSINEO

(Marymount Manhattan College). Additional Playwriting credits include Jesus stole my birth control (Secret Theatre), The Microwave Play (Secret Theatre), Two Hearts (Manhattan Repertory Theatre) and Bad Beans at (Geva Theatre). Directing Credits include Posers at (Manhattan Repertory Theatre) and Carrier Pigeon (Theatre for the New City).

BELOVED HUSBAND

PAULA GAIL BENSON

(*The year is 1990. Norton Baskin enters from stage left, approaching center stage. The location is a shabbily elegant hotel lobby on the eastern Florida coast, with rattan chairs, a table, and a straw rug. The lighting overhead indicates a slowly rotating fan. He wears a light-colored suit and straw fedora, which he takes off and holds to his chest, as if greeting guests he does not know, but to whom he extends old-fashioned courtesy.*)

NORTON BASKIN:

Good day to you. Please come inside and rest from your travels. I'm sure we can provide some refreshments . . .

(*He pauses, as if a guest has asked him a question.*)

You say my face is familiar? Well, I admit being in a movie once. In 1983. But, you'd have to have watched closely to see my scene.

. . .

The film's name? *Cross Creek*. Based on a memoir by Mrs. Marjorie Kinnan Rawlings. A fine writer. Won the Pulitzer Prize for her novel, *The Yearling*. Found her voice in the 1920s, when she and her first husband moved to a rural orange grove. The stories she told about the local inhabitants became more fascinating than rewriting tired gothic romances.

How did I get in the film? Well… I started as a technical consultant. Matter of fact, the message in the credits thanking me for my contributions got more screen time than my acting.

You see, I was Mrs. Rawlings' second husband. Not that our life together was much like the movie. Good casting by those Hollywood folks of that fine-looking Peter Coyote to play me. But, even he admitted, you have to act the script, whether or not it mirrors real life.

In this case, it didn't. Marjorie didn't leave her first husband to come to Cross Creek. They bought that orange grove together. Mr. Rawlings just never took to the lifestyle like she did. Committing to Cross Creek meant embracing solitude. Marjorie did that gladly. Maybe she could appreciate society's outsiders because she felt like one herself.

We were very different, she and I. She grew up with all the opportunities and advantages. Educated for a literary life. And inside, she had that innate stubbornness to keep striving, even when she likely wouldn't reach her goals.

After her divorce, she kept the orange grove. Stayed in Cross Creek. She refused to let others define her life. But, she craved reassurance, whether or not she would admit it.

. . .

Kept asking me to marry her. Not for companionship or caretaking. Just from time to time, she needed the quiet voice saying – you're on the right path. The gentle hand on her back that strengthened her spine and made her stand taller. Her own resolve, just reinforced.

She had all the words. I was just a poor Alabama boy who grew up in a house full of siblings. I had no illusion of attending college. Never rooted for the Crimson Tide or the War Eagles. My uncle worked in an Atlanta hotel. He got me a job and I became a hotel man, working my way up from clerk to security to management. Ultimately bought this place of my own.

I knew how to be useful to people. How to read their needs while giving them their space.

Maybe that's what Marjorie liked best about me. She didn't interfere in my hotel business and I didn't try to write her books.

Except, after she passed on, I had to ensure her legacy -- her words continuing.

I wrote the memorial inscription for her grave. "Through her writings, she endeared herself to the people of the world."

When my time comes, it will be enough to lie beside her, with only my name on the stone.

Of course, it would be pleasant to have "Beloved Husband" after my name. I think she might have considered me that.

. . .

Now, you just take a seat and rest. I'll check about those refreshments.

(*Norton Baskin exits to order the refreshments.*)

A legislative attorney and former law librarian, Paula Gail Benson's short stories have appeared in the Bethlehem Writers Roundtable; Kings River Life; Mystery Times Ten 2013; A Tall Ship, a Star, and Plunder; A Shaker of Margaritas: That Mysterious Woman; Fish or Cut Bait: a Guppy Anthology; Love in the Lowcountry; and Heartbreaks and Half-truths. She regularly blogs with others about writing mysteries at the Stiletto Gang and Writers Who Kill. Her short story, "A Matter of Honor," co-authored with New York Times Bestselling thriller writer Robert Dugoni, is in Killer Nashville Noir: Cold Blooded. In addition to short stories, she writes and directs one act musicals for her church's drama ministry. Paula's website is http://paulagailbenson.com.

I BELIEVE IN A WORLD OF POSSIBILITIES

DAVID LANGE

The Loch Ness Monster, space aliens, and everything in between. I believe. It's as simple as that. And because I do, you discount my position on every other topic under the sun. I have become irrelevant... in your eyes. More's the pity, for I might have opened your mind to a world of wonders and limitless possibilities.

As a child, I was an avid reader of any book or article concerning my favorite sea monster, Nessie, the famed monster of Loch Ness. In my youth, on vacation in the United Kingdom, our tour director found me out and began loaning me copies of booklets on the monster, in preparation for our visit to the Highlands of Scotland. I eagerly read each booklet and pamphlet, returning the material the following morning. Our planned Loch Ness "drive-by" transitioned into an unscheduled stop and I believe, to this day, the agenda modification was a gift from our kind guide to a young boy. I went to the lake's edge and placed my hand in the cold water. It was a magical moment. I scanned the surface of the lake for any ripple that might betray the presence of a fast-traveling sea serpent. The world was ripe with possibilities. There was hope that tomorrow might be more exciting than today as the unexpected and unknown progressed from fiction to fact. Mankind has made countless discoveries over the ages. Why do you doubt the presence of a prehistoric creature in Loch Ness?

Why do you doubt that Sasquatch wanders the vast woodlands of the Pacific Northwest? And you doubt the existence of extraterrestrials yet you've failed to establish the borders of the universe. In this infinite expanse of space, I see infinite possibilities. Do you see a cold and lifeless vacuum?

I know. I was to outgrow these "childish" notions, casting them aside as fairy tales and myths, on that very day that I stopped believing in Santa Claus. Are you sure that I did? What if I didn't? Am I now a candidate for referral to a mental health clinic? I assure you, there are many in greater need than I; let them profit from these resources, I have other matters that need attending and those matters rely upon a youthful optimism and hope that the world might be more than we imagine and that, in life, we may do more than simply live and die.

Offer me proof? you say. Why? Why do I need to prove anything? Perhaps you should prove that I'm wrong. I've been down this road before. You point to studies, and formulas, and those pesky laws of physics. You tell me how they've scanned the entire volume of Loch Ness with sonar sweeps, sampled the waters for unrecognizable DNA traces, sent countless robotic submersibles equipped with advanced camera systems to scan the depths; they've exhausted all modern research methods... and yet nothing. No sign of a monster. I am fascinated by all of this. My mind remains unchanged. You see, I know something that you don't. Mankind's entire volume of knowledge is based upon observation and experimentation. We've sampled, and measured; quantified, and documented. We've established thresholds for certainty and we have promoted theories to facts. I applaud all these efforts. I have a scientific mind. I also have a philosophical mind. And I know that our tomes of irreputable facts are born of our fanatical desire to control our surroundings and predict the future. We shut out the truths we simply don't wish to hear. I do not.

Who's to say that the laws of gravity might not flip head over heels every billion years? Newton's apple might one day accelerate upward into the sky. The sun might radiate a beautiful purple light and man might walk upon the surface of the water as he now treads upon the firm pavement beneath his feet. Do you believe a man can walk on water? Do you believe a man once did? I hope I have not offended, but I ask you, please, to consider all that you believe and all that you do not. What is real? What is possible? I am quite content that you should shape the world in the manner you choose; I won't deny you this. I will, however, respectfully, request that you allow me to shape my world as I see fit—to apply my own brush strokes upon the empty canvas that I have been given.

I've met people who have seen Sasquatch. They've told me so. I have no reason to doubt them, nor do I feel any compulsion to prove them wrong. I've read stories about "monster" sightings on Loch Ness, and upon a number of other bodies of water. I understand that if you look hard enough–if your search is that desperate–your senses might betray you. I get it. But why should I crush hope? Why should I doubt the fantastic when the fantastic makes this world that much more exhilarating? In the boundless reaches of space, I have no doubt there are beings of equal, and most certainly, greater intellect than our own exalted human race. They might, occasionally, desire to take a vacation to our planet, and dip their appendages into the cool waters of Loch Ness, much as I did. Why not? Perhaps they did lend a hand during the construction of Stone Henge, the great pyramids of Egypt, and who knows what else. My world view will never depend upon believing that these things are true. My world view absolutely depends upon my conceding that they might be.

In 1938, an expedition purposely sent to uncover the facts behind a wild rumor discovered a monster of a fish that was supposed to have gone extinct some 66 million years ago. Somehow, the coelacanth eluded our discovery through all recorded history. Similarly, the okapi, a mammal of great stature that looks like a strange cross between a zebra and giraffe, is now familiar to most naturalists. Yet this large creature remained hidden for centuries and was deemed a preposterous myth until its discovery by a British explorer, Sir Harry Hamilton Johnston, in 1901. Fiction becomes fact. Legends inspire our imagination and those brave enough to step beyond the borders of our current understanding are often hailed as heroes... or fools. I applaud the heroes and the fools; I cheer for those who seek and those who believe. Perhaps, one day, someone will sing my praises?

I'll not hold my breath. When I lay down for my final rest, I can assure you that I shall do so with hope and an unbroken faith that Shakespeare's Hamlet was not far off the mark when he advised Horatio that there are more things in Heaven and Earth than are dreamt of in your philosophy. I believe in a world of possibilities.

David Lange was born and grew up on Long Island, New York. A graduate of the United States Air Force Academy, he served for 30 years as an Active Duty officer in the United States Air Force before retiring in 2018. Colonel Lange is a decorated combat veteran, and flew numerous combat, combat support, and humanitarian relief missions during his career. He was awarded the prestigious Institute of Navigation Superior Achievement Award in recognition of his lifelong accomplishments as a practicing navigator. David loves sharing stories of hope and inspiration and, in 2020, he published his memoir, "Quest: My Journey Through La Mancha."

CLOUDED

AMANDA MONTONI

SARAH is going through a bit of an identity crisis. She feels lost. Stuck. Clouded. She doesn't know where or when her next step will be. She lives with her husband, CHUCK, and confesses her innermost thoughts and feelings to him.

SARAH. How am I doing? ...You know the feeling when there's heat in the room and the air is stagnant so your face feels like it's expanding and shrinking at the same time? Like your skull is being crushed and your eyeballs are popping out of their sockets and all you want to do is let them go, but you can't? Cause they're stuck there? Well, that's how I'm doing right now. As I was looking out the window this morning, I thought of what my life used to be. Simple. Happy. Content. I used to be able to look up at the sky and see clarity. Everything was so clear up there. Now, all I see is uncertainty. What has happened to me, Chuck? The clouds used to be hearts and elephants and unicorns in my eyes. They would take me with them through the sun and leave me with beams shooting out of my body in every direction. I was so sure of my next step. I was unstoppable. I was happy to be alive. I would look back at the grass below my feet and think "wow, the sky has a spirit." I used to have a spirit. Now, the clouds are just puffs of rain moving along, forever morphing, trying to set themselves free. I'm the rain trapped in the puffs of myself. Eyeballs popping out but never escaping. Let me be free. Let me be free, Chuck. Stop it. Make it stop. (*She pauses and glances out the window.*) The clouds are so low in the sky today.

Amanda Montoni has been involved in the world of theater for most of her life. She started acting in the plays and musicals at school, and has been hit by the theater bug ever since. Being a co-founder of the Royal Star Theater company in Queens, she is heavily involved in bringing theater to the community. Amanda grew up with a love for the arts, dancing her way through life, and has been given the great opportunity to be a dance and theater educator for almost 10 years. Since she became an established Choreographer and Director, it was only natural that she start to write for the theater as well.

LOBSTER OF MY LIFE

AN EXCERPT FROM THE ONE-ACT RADIO PLAY, "BOILED BREAKUP"

AMANDA MONTONI

LARRY is a lobster boiling to death in a pot of hot water. He sees his time with LIELLE, his ex-girlfriend, flash before his eyes.

LARRY. You know when you die, there's this white light people talk about? Or for others, their life flashes before their eyes? Well, for me, those are just more human legends. I remembered Lielle. After we got caught in the net, we ended up in this giant square filled with saltwater in the middle of this incredibly bright place where the humans came to get their food. It was incredibly terrifying. We were plopped into a tank filled with other lobsters with nowhere to go. Stuck there. Crawling on top of each other. Our claws tied up. Whatever they had us in was nothing compared to what we saw out across from us. Fish. All kinds of fish wrapped in plastic on a plate. Dead. One by one they were picked off by their hungry humans, and one by one the lobsters imprisoned with us were picked off until Lielle and I were the only two left...That is what I saw before I died. Lielle and I, surrounded by dead fish, but most importantly we were surrounded by Lielle's hope. She was right. There was a fighting chance we could have made it out, and I wasn't going to be the one to take that chance away from her. I *am* too much, and proudly so. The "lobsters mate for life human crab shit," as she put it, might be legend, but I do believe that Lielle was, quite frankly, the lobster of my life.

> While involved in a playwriting/podcast group, Amanda Montoni was given a writing prompt to write a break-up scene. Not having any ideas, she stumbled upon the quote from the popular T.V. sitcom, F.R.I.E.N.D.S., in which one of the characters mentions the old tale that lobsters mate for life. Amanda immediately went to work, researching if lobsters do indeed mate for life. Turns out she found that was a myth. This saddened her, as she is a romantic, but gave her the subject for her scene. Larry and Lielle have been dating for 2 weeks. When they are about to be cooked to death, Lielle breaks Larry's heart and pops the naive bubble he was living in. She educates him on the truth about lobsters, crushing the human legends Larry believed in with his whole heart. See, he wanted a wife, kids, a house, the ideal dream of a family. With out giving too much of the play away, Larry ends up being the extraordinary, selfless creature he always strived to be. He dies knowing he helped the person he loved most and happy that he spent his last moments making and helping an unexpected friend. Larry dies a hero.

PUNXSUTAWNEY PHIL IS SICK OF THIS SHIT: A MONOLOGUE FOR A PISSED-OFF DEITY

HAYLEY ST. JAMES

PHIL, a groundhog, is sitting on a stool. He wears a red bow tie and looks extremely cute but ALSO VERY PISSED OFF.

PHIL

So.

It's February 2nd. Again.

You all know what that means.

I'm supposed to come out of my burrow in podunk Punxsutawney, Pennsylvania, and if I see my shadow, there's six more weeks of winter. If I don't, spring'll come early.

Well, tough shit. This year, I don't want to come out. Leave me alone.

There is literally a blizzard hitting the northeast, and I do not want to fucking go outside.

I have enough backlogged on my Netflix queue to last me the entire week, let alone my holiday.

PHIL crosses his arms in a huff.

Yeah. It's my holiday. I deserve a break this year. 2020 was bad enough. I DIDN'T SEE MY SHADOW IN 2020. And look at what happened the rest of the year.

Okay, a Pennsylvania boy becoming president thanks to our state turning blue was nice. But STILL. 2020? BAD.

You know, on the surface I look like an ordinary groundhog.

PHIL starts posing like a runway model.

Cute little face, cute stubby body. These utterly adorable paws! Am I a squirrel or a beaver? Both? Neither? Whatever I am, I'm adorable. Iconic, even. But inside this sweet furry exterior is an ancient, all-powerful being capable of controlling time and weather!

PHIL looks straight out at his audience.

That's right.

I control the seasons, bitch.

In ancient times I was worshipped as a deity by long-forgotten native civilizations on lands that have shifted and changed with the millennia! In those days I made sure the seasons ran like clockwork, along with all the other deities of seasonal change. Me and Persephone? Besties. Yeah, the holy pantheons of the world are all actually quite chummy with one another. Too bad mankind started pitting wars against each other over whose deities were correct.

Spoiler alert, y'all: we're all correct. Stop the holy wars, people.

I should add.

That movie, with Bill Murray? The one they turned into a Tim Minchin musical? That shit's the closest the media has ever gotten to understanding my powers.

Controlling time is just one aspect of controlling seasons.

So of course I'd make a time loop to teach a rude white man how to be nice to people.

So anyway. There was once an age where I was running the show in the seasons department... making the leaves fall from the trees and the snow pile up and the grass grow and the sun shine.

And then... as it so often happens... the white people came and destroyed everything.

You guessed it! These fuckers gentrified me! And it's been hell for little old me ever since!

PHIL gets up from his stool and starts pacing and gesticulating with his paws as he continues to rant.

Every year they crowd around me in my hole and watch over me with a million cameras... the lack of PRIVACY! It's UPSETTING! So of course I see my shadow most of the time - with the camera flashes how can there NOT BE A SHADOW?

If I had my space I could tap back into my ancient magic and give you all the seasons as they should be... but I can't do that either. Because the white people also caused global warming, and put a damper on my powers.

So now I can only do...

PHIL gestures vaguely.

What everyone thinks I'm supposed to do. The "see my shadow six more weeks of winter" bullshit.

PHIL sits back down on his stool.

So yeah. I'm pissed off. And rightfully so.

If you just gave me a fucking year off and gave me some respect, maybe the world can get back to normal.

So while you're at it, respect the land you live on. It doesn't belong to you. You live on stolen land that ancestrally belongs to native people who were here first. It's sacred.

So I'm sorry, people.

I need the day off. Maybe next year.

PHIL gets up off the stool and exits the stage. Lights down.

Hayley St. James (they/them) is a Boston-born, mostly-New York-based playwright and performer, and a graduate of Marymount Manhattan College's class of 2020. A non-binary lesbian on the autism spectrum, they are deeply passionate about seeing themselves and their communities represented truthfully in all media, theatre first and foremost. In their theatrical work, they strive to marry authentic representation with hyper-theatrical, surreal, meta, and intimate twists. They also have a thing for imaginary friends, ghosts, aliens, and well-handled pop culture references.

Their plays include "For Leonora, Or, Companions," a play with puppetry elements about life and love on the autism and LBGTQ+ spectrum; "Shrike and Magpie," a ten-minute jewel heist comedy caper with a dash of lesbian intrigue; and their Queerantine '20 Cycle, a deeply intimate series of plays exploring touch, longing, time, and routine in the age of Corona, anxiety, hope, fear, the generation gap between millennials and their boomer parents during the 2020 Election, and the life-changing magic of David Bowie. The Queerantine '20 Cycle consists of "A Godawful Small Affair," "It's Confusing, These Days," and "The Last Night of January."

I WAS A BOND GIRL

ANITA HAAS

"What's your name, honey?"

"Spelt. Claudia Spelt. And yours?"

"Bond. James Bond."

Then, Sean Connery swung his long, lean body into the driver's seat of the convertible, put the top up, and leaned over to kiss me.

That was my tiny, one-line part, in *Doctor No*. I was so proud of it. After six long years of modeling, I had finally broken into the world of cinema.

Of course, at that time, no one could have predicted the enormous success the film would later enjoy, that there would be so many sequels, and the great prestige that being a Bond Girl would have. I was just thrilled to be a part of it.

The only child of a British office worker and a Spanish seamstress, my parents always believed in me. After years of courses and classes; acting, singing, dance, make-up, I was ready. My agent was ecstatic when I took my mother's maiden name, going from Victoria Smith to Vicky Gomez. He said it sounded sexy and exotic to British ears.

When I first laid eyes on the script, I fell in love with the role of Miss Taro, so I dyed my hair, wore false eyelashes, lost three kilos, and squeezed my generous bosom into a push-up bra to fit the part. What a disappointment when I was given the smaller part of Claudia Spelt. But it wasn't bad for a start. Not bad at all. I had recently turned 25, and all my hard work was finally paying off.

Dressed in slinky attire, I was the subject of dozens of photos. Everyone said I was the prettiest girl in the cast, even prettier than Ursula Andress, the star. Advertising companies fought over me. But I rejected them all. I had slaved away in modeling for too many years. Now I wanted to be an actress.

Terence Young, the director, loved me. A crew member confided that they had chosen Ursula Andress for the starring role only because they were convinced a blonde would help sell the film! Can you believe it?

At the end of the shoot, they paid me, and then I didn't hear a peep from anyone. Even Margaret Polly and Philippa Wayne, actresses I had become friendly with, became distant, like they knew something. They stopped answering my calls.

I started to worry.

I will never forget opening night. They hadn't invited me, which I found strange, but I thought maybe it was just an oversight and went with my parents and some neighbors. Confusion reigned in the lobby, and they didn't want to let us in. Nobody believed I was actually in the film. Then I saw one of the director's assistants and waved to him. His look of surprise and embarrassment worried me, especially when, instead of coming to us, he ran off to speak to someone else. But a moment later they let us in. I made sure to give the security people a dirty look.

My whole body tingled. I couldn't concentrate on the film at all. When it was time for my scene, I elbowed my parents on either side of me. James Bond enters the hotel lobby, and a beautiful receptionist tells him that the car he ordered had arrived, but not without giving him a significant look, meaning a sexy, exotic girl (me), was waiting for him in that car.

This was it!

But it wasn't. The film jumped to the next scene.

I clung to the hope that they had placed it later on. But as the film progressed, I had to accept the fact that it had been cut.

My parents were silent as we left the cinema. Through the blur of my tears, I saw Young's assistant apologizing profusely, "They forgot to inform you. If it's any consolation, it wasn't the only scene cut. The film was just too long." My dad said something about bad manners, and we caught a taxi home.

It took me a while to recover.

To start with, my agent told me some modeling agencies had accused him of lying about my appearance in *Doctor. No*. There was no way we could prove I had actually played a part, and it was even more humiliating to admit the truth.

I became depressed and stopped eating, then I went to the other extreme and put on loads of weight.

Shortly after, my agent informed me that it was no longer in his best interest to represent me. I was already twenty-seven, and a new crop of young, thin models was coming up behind me. My mother got me a job with her in the glove factory, and every now and then I landed a gig as an extra, hoping I might be rediscovered. But it didn't do more than put a few pennies in my pocket and more agony in my heart.

I never missed a Bond film. It was a form of deliberate self-torture. Every time I saw one, I suffered for weeks.

Soon the tributes, festivals, conventions, and retrospectives began. They invited me to one. I was touched, but It turned out to be one of the worst experiences of my life. All the attendees glowed with beauty and style, talking incessantly about their careers and new projects. "And you, Vicky? What are you up to?" They never invited me again.

Of course, I knew all those gorgeous starlets were under the same pressure I was, or at least I know it now. They made up their lives, like they made up their faces, boasting about roles, influential friendships, and popularity while my magazines informed me of scandal, failure, divorce, depression, and addiction. It is a brutal, unforgiving world that I desperately wanted to be part of.

The next year I married a neighbor and entered motherhood, that last card so many attractive women play when they fear they will never succeed at anything. But after the initial congratulations, baby showers, and a promise of a happy, wall-papered domestic life, reality kicked in and it fizzled out into a snotty prison, reeking of diapers and my husband's sweaty overalls. I expanded several dress sizes and soon divorced. I developed a taste for gin and other things. That was cute Claudia Spelt at forty.

The judge decided to let my ex keep our son, and rightly so, I suppose. But admitting that doesn't make it easier. They left London and I haven't seen them since. I cried every day and drank every night for a year.

I became that pathetic, drunk woman you see in seedy neighborhood pubs. It was normal to hear me shouting in front of a group of amused and disgusted faces, "I was a Bond Girl! I was! It's true!"

Margaret Polly, Philippa Wayne, and that cold fish, Ursula Andress.

Of course, I knew in my head that they were not to blame for my situation, but I needed something to focus on, an objective, a mission. I decided to murder them.

I didn't have to do much research since I had been following their careers for years. I knew where they lived, what circles they moved in, even where they shopped and which hairdressers attended to them.

I took my time. I was living with my senile, widowed mother, and when she watched the telly in the sitting room, I was at the table, planning. Deciding just when, where, and how to go about it was a lot of fun. The most important thing was to let sufficient time pass between each crime so no one would make the connection.

My first victim would be Margaret. Her role could easily have been cut instead of mine because it didn't affect the story either. Although she had never done much to brag about, her attitude towards me had always been superior, and even more so after my disgrace. I suppose she realized she couldn't benefit from our friendship.

To my delight, I discovered they were looking for a waitress in the coffee shop where Margaret breakfasted. So many years had passed and I had changed so much, she would never recognize me.

It all went smoothly. I mixed rat poison in her coffee, stirred it, and it dissolved immediately, the taste disguised by all the saccharin she added. The next day I read about it in the newspaper. They said she had died of a heart attack while walking back home. Apparently, she had always had a weak heart. Lucky for me!

Since it had all been so easy, I decided to wait only two years before killing Philippa, as opposed to the five I had originally planned on.

Something strange was happening to me. After Margaret's death, I began to lose weight, and I started going to the gym. And one fine day, I gave up booze. I had never felt so good, both inside and out. I was a curvy, attractive, mature woman with a Latin touch that got people's attention! It wasn't long before I had a new boyfriend.

I came up with a more creative way of killing, nothing to do with poison. Repeating the same crime would have bored me. True crime stories became my exclusive viewing and reading. I wanted this murder to be spectacular, cinematographic, like fiddling the brakes on her sports car, or putting a rattlesnake in her bed.

I remembered that one of the murder attempts on James Bond in our film included a tarantula! What a sensational way to die!

At that time, I had a dopey boyfriend who loved to please me. I never found out how or where he got the spider. The important thing is that he did. No questions asked.

I didn't hide it in Philippa's bed. Too predictable, and a bit difficult, too. I followed her on a trip to her hairdresser, and having noted that she liked to leave the passenger window open a crack, I snuck up to it with the bag, glanced left and right, and dropped the fat, hairy beast on the seat.

The wait seemed endless. Finally, Philippa came out, looking quite elegant, I must admit. She got in and started the engine. I don't know if the spider bit her, or if, out of fright, she lost control of the car. In any case, after swerving around a bit, she crashed into a building under construction, and the car exploded. What scriptwriter could come up with something so good?

I left my boyfriend shortly after. He was a good guy and obedient, but he wasn't adding anything to my life anymore. I started fantasizing about murder all day long. I was getting creative and ambitious, researching and inventing all manner of killing. The victims would all be from the cast and crew of the film; technicians, actors, maybe even Sean Connery himself, with a beretta, like the one he used as Bond!

But first I had to kill Ursula Andress.

In our film, Ursula had played the part of a shell collector, so I figured drowning would be the most poetic death for her. Relatively little time had passed since Philippa, but I had so many great ideas and so many people to kill, that I had to hurry!

My movie magazines informed me that a tribute was being organized for Ursula in the Spanish coastal city of Almeria. They were awarding her for her participation in *Red Sun*, one of those spaghetti westerns filmed there in the sixties. I had to accept some pretty bad conditions to get a job in her hotel, with such short notice.

My Spanish was rusty, but no worse than that of many of the immigrants on staff. I wrote my script and rehearsed my part like the star I should have been. How wrong I had been all those years ago! My real career as an actress was just beginning!

The plan was to sneak into her room at night, strangle her, force her to recognize me, and then finish her off in the bathtub.

My earlier victims had died without having their offenses explained to them. This time would be different.

"Don't you remember me, Ursula?" I practiced in the mirror of the hotel laundry room. "I'm little Vicky Gomez, the actress in *Doctor No* whose scene was cut."

An inexplicable energy rose from my gut to my throat and took over my whole body. My head was spinning and my expression reflected in the mirror had changed so much that I couldn't even recognize myself.

"Are you sure you don't remember me, Miss Andress?" I heard my voice shouting as if from a great distance. "Little Vicky Gomez. And now you are going to die!"

Suddenly the door opened behind me. The mirror reflected three uniformed men. I panicked. This was not in the script!

"No!" I shouted again and again, but they had already handcuffed me from behind and were forcing me out of the room.

I don't remember anything after that. Only my own voice shrieking, "I was a Bond Girl!!! I was! It's true!"

Anita Haas is a differently-abled Canadian writer and teacher based in Madrid, Spain. She has published books on film, two novelettes, a short story collection, and articles, poems and fiction in both English and Spanish.

Some publications her fiction has appeared in include Falling Star Magazine, The Tulane Review, Literary Brushstrokes, The Zodiac Review, River Poets Journal, Scarlet Leaf Review, Terror House Magazine, Wink and Adelaide Magazine. She spends her free time watching films, and enjoying tapas and flamenco with her writer husband and two cats.

THE FOOL ON THE HILL

WILLIAM JOHN ROSTRON

Background: A middle-aged father is taking his oldest child to tour a prestigious, but small liberal arts college. A cynic by nature, he is trying to determine what is best for his child and whether the education provided is worth the money to be spent. While on the tour, he ponders all these questions.

"Who is more foolish? The fool, or the one who follows him?" I remember that quote from when I was in college. I think it was maybe humorist Will Rogers who said it about a political situation. However, it might have been a more serious journalist writing about Adolf Hitler. I just can't seem to remember. However, the fact that I remember hearing it at all speaks to the quality of education I received at a public college.

Okay, so what am I doing at this costly liberal arts college tour with my son? Do I really have to spend a quarter of a million dollars on his education? I mean, I turned out fine. Yet here I am, trudging up this hill on this endless tour to see one beautiful building after another. They want my money, and to that end, they have sent a 19-year-old to lead me. Is he the fool, or am I the fool for following him and allowing him to seduce the money from my bank accounts?

But there are others with us. I wonder about each of their stories. Next to us is a father who is very blatantly sporting a Harvard school ring. Didn't he give enough money to the alumni fund for his kid to be a legacy admission? Or is he just checking out some safe schools? Alternatively, maybe his kid is just a dumb shit.

Then there is that couple over there that are just perfect. Do you know what I mean? They are the couple with the perfect children. Come on; you must know a family just like them—we all do. Of course, they have one boy and one girl—they planned it that way. These two cherubs never get in trouble, do all their chores, always do their homework, never answer back, never fight with each other, and are generally ... well ... perfect. They make me face my own inadequacies. I mean, how have I failed so badly. In fact, they are right now telling the whole crowd of us about their daughter, the yearbook editor, school paper reporter, captain of the girls' lacrosse team, and I guess, future prom queen. I look over at my son. He is not even looking at all the beautiful buildings but rather incessantly starring at the ground as we walk.

What am I doing here? Yes, the buildings are so much more beautiful than the cookie-cutter structures of my state school. If he goes here maybe he will make networking connections with some rich and famous friends? Perhaps it will be worth the money. Or am I being a fool? Where the hell did I hear that quote? I can't take anymore. While we take a short break at the top of this hill, I think I'll google it. Oh shit, so that's who said it!

To take my mind off of what I just found out, I decided to ask my son why he was looking at the ground? I only half-listened at first but then became enthralled by his answer. He told me that at every school we visited, we looked at the beautiful buildings. All of the tour guides talked about how outstanding their programs were. However, my son had decided to look at their sidewalks instead. "It's simple," he told me. "They are blowing you over with the fluff, but I have a different gauge to measure quality. As we walk around every campus, I look at sidewalks—that's where you see the truth. If they care about their students, they make sure there are no cracks for them to trip on and get hurt. It shows their priorities, not their outer shell. So while you were looking up, I was looking down.

It does make sense to me now. Especially in light of the pretentious, pseudo-intellectual quote with which I started this whole rant. I am the fool who is leading around my son, thinking he has no deep thoughts. I am also the fool who is being led by this sophomore who is dazzling me with knowledge of the beautiful buildings. I think I will just let my son decide. He really shouldn't be listening to someone like me who thinks they are quoting someone important... when they are actually quoting Obi-wan Kenobi to Luke Skywalker in the very first Star Wars movie.

The author recently completed a trilogy of novels steeped in the late 20th and early 21st centuries' music and culture. Band in the Wind, Sound of Redemption, and Brotherhood of Forever have received critical acclaim from Writers Digest, the Online Book Club Review, and many other reviewers. These books have found readership on four continents (North America, Europe, Australia, and Asia).

In the past, he has published over two dozen non-fiction articles in newspapers and magazines. These writings included four full-page op-eds in New York Newsday. He was also presented an award by Nelson DeMille for his historical fiction short story, "The Last Artifact." Recently, his short pieces have in published in ten Red Penguin anthologies:

Three of his short pieces were accepted into the Visible Ink anthologies in 2018, 2019, and 2020. Each year, a dozen works are chosen for reading and presentation on stage in New York City. In 2018, "Pretty Flamingo" was given this honor. As an encore, "In the Garden of Eden" was performed in 2019. In 2020, his short work "Ava's Bubble" was read by Tony and Emmy nominee Victor Garber on a nationally televised streaming show. All of these are available for viewing on www.williamjohnrostron.com.

In his previous career, the author instructed students from the ages of 9 to 90. In his life, he taught elementary school, middle school, high school, college, adult education, and teacher training. He holds degrees from Queens College, Stony Brook University, and Long Island University.

Born and raised in Queens, NY, William John Rostron now splits his time between his home on Long Island and traveling the country in his Tiffin motorhome. When not writing, he is busy completing a bucket list of travel adventures. In the past 16 years, he and his wife Marilyn have traveled 120,000 miles. These journeys have taken them to the 48 contiguous states, 133 national parks, all 30 major league baseball stadiums, 154 cities and towns, two Canadian provinces, and a variety of unusual experiences and locations. Many of these locations have served as backgrounds for his books.

He presently working on a novel, Lost in the Wind, and an anthology, A Flamingo Under the Carousel.

SMART

A MONOLOGUE FROM THE PLAY "STANDARD."

SAGE HOLLOWAY

SOPHIE. Yeah. Smart. That's me... Except I've been thinking. And what is it that makes me so "smart"? I filled in some bubbles and they gave me a number and I guess that number is supposed to define me. I'm supposed to love this number that made me number one, made me somehow the best.

But who decides that? Who writes the damn test questions anyway? And why do they get to define intelligence? I just have a hard time loving that number when I know how many people are destroyed by theirs. I don't think it's fair. The more I think about it, the more it just isn't fair.

(there is a considerable pause as she debates whether she should say this; she does.)

Are you ever thinking, and your brain just goes from one thing to another faster than you're really aware? Like I'll think about cats, and then, I don't know, I'll think about how cats have moms–just like people. And then, like, imagine a cat wishing her daughter good luck on her test day. And how funny it would be if a cat was grounded or something... and then my brain stops. Like it's only built to think in one direction and cats with parents isn't right. And I don't think I was built that way. No, I think I was trained. Like all these tests that we're told define us, they only measure that one direction of thinking. People who score low, maybe they just think in so many directions that it's hard to control and maybe they're just as smart. Or smarter. I mean, I've known you, what, two days? And you've already taught me so much. How can I be smarter than you? How could I possibly be above you? What if I'm not? And I'm just the best at filling in bubbles? Making my mark heavy and dark. Following the instructions on the test packet. Not making any stray marks in the margins. What if we are missing all of those stray marks? What if we are missing what really matters?

Creativity. Thinking in different directions. Why don't I have that? I'm like this gear in a giant machine, spinning in a single direction and never stopping, or really making anything. Just maintaining. Oh my God, maintaining, like you said. We aren't a productive society. We don't make anything. We just maintain.

> Sage is from Kenosha Wisconsin and loves it. She lives in Boston now, where she studies film and TV and psychology. She'll graduate soon and then she doesn't really know what's next, but that's okay. If you liked this monologue, reach out to her on her website or her Instagram @sageholla. Love ya!

SO THIS IS RECOVERY?
A MONOLOGUE FROM THE PLAY "ED"

SAGE HOLLOWAY

FIONA. I remember this one time, in like fifth grade. I don't even know what I was doing or if I had school that day or what, but I just felt so guilty, for no reason. And I had this little Hello Kitty journal that I'd use to write silly stories and sometimes I'd do a diary entry as if it was a habit, all "Dear Diary, it's January sixth." And I just remember that day, feeling so bad and not knowing why. And I decided to use that to, like, write a story about a girl who fucked up so bad and maybe found retribution by the end? I don't fucking know...

So I started creating these scenarios, like accidentally killing my hamster, or dropping my brother's birthday cake. Stuff I didn't do. And none of it seemed bad enough to warrant this fictional version of me feeling that bad. So, I put it down and I went downstairs and ate a bagel. And then I had another bagel, because we had two types of bagel and I wanted one of each. And then I wanted something sweet to balance the taste, so I finished off a pint of ice cream. And then I wanted something fruity, so I ate these little candies I had gotten from Easter. And then I guess I probably painted my nails or watched Disney Channel and went to bed.

. . .

Even now, I don't know where that guilt came from, but I still feel it. I'm getting better. I'm gaining weight. My cheeks aren't puffy and swollen anymore. My hair is healthier, my nails are stronger. I haven't thrown up in weeks.

But I haven't found a new way to purge that guilt.

I don't know where it came from but I'm starting to understand that eating is how I fill my body with shame, and I found such a great way of getting rid of it. Clear body, clear mind.

So this is recovery. This?

"So this is recovery?" is an excerpt from the play *ED*, which has been performed at Bradford High School, Indian Trail High School, and the Rhode Center for the Arts in Kenosha, WI. In 2017, *ED* competed in the Wisconsin State Theater Festival, taking home multiple acting awards as well as Critic's Choice Award. Most recently, *ED* was adapted into a full-length virtual production for Boston University Stage Troupe's Theater in Action, raising over $1400 for Project Heal, an organization that increases accessibility to eating disorder treatment. *ED* is a dark comedy that follows Fiona, a teenager in treatment for bulimia, through her tragic story of recovery. Email shollow@bu.edu for access to the full script, and/or reach out on Instagram @sageholla!

FRUIT FLIES

ANNABEL WEBSTER

Shoshone, Idaho. morning. SPARKLE is standing on a dark stage, wearing a backpack and a very mid-2000s pre-teen outfit. Her clothes are kind of ill-fitting and dirty. She is awkward and self-conscious. She looks up.

SPARKLE

I was conceived in a cornfield at the filer fair

in filer idaho

dry september night the moon was out no stars in the sky

just the hot bright bulbs of carnival rides the smell of burning oil and manure

my mother beautiful 16 invincible head cheerleader, evangelical bombshell

had a thing for the ride operators

methed out old men drunkenly piecing together ancient airplane parts staring at young girls passing through their gates strapped down and helpless

to these giant spinning angel machines, ancient light up god robots

the americana stone henge

mama thought the ride operators were like biblical shepherds

herding trailers of kamikaze & zipper shepherding them to fair ground holy lands

across america

cigarettes of frankincense, he smells like myrrh

glassy eyes shining haloes in the dark

she leads them to the cornfield at the edge of the fair, past the 4H tents

and gold rush photo booths, she lifts up her dress

she shows them her girlish 1950s housewife undies, she says can you smell me

from here

like a yuppy siren she leads them away from the brightness of carnival ride into

the dark, cornfield shines black as she smiles

disappearing into the crop

she'd fuck them there, her cries indistinguishable from the squealing of

slaughtered pigs the grunts of a petting zoo

and they come

FRUIT FLIES

inside

of

her

they pat her on the head

say free rides from now on

and leave her in the dark surrounded by corn stocks and daddy long leg

panties around her knees she thinks thank you, god

thank you for this blessing this immaculate conception

and lies there the dark sky washing over her

listening to the death squeal slaughter music of the pigs in the distance

and now i am here

i am nothing like my mother

shy girl, quiet people at school say my hair is greasy and i smell bad

i walk home alone on the highway, no one can see my

eyes, my glasses are too dirty

fruit flies land on my shoulders, their tiny wings become mine

please fly me home fruit flies

i only inherited one good thing from my mother

i can hear the call of god and i can smell him, ancient

and breathing, like mold, like mildew, like my basement

like the spine of an old book

echoing from the lava tubes behind my house

ANNABEL WEBSTER

i feel him enter me through the dust storms pouring through my window

coating me in sand

i am a monument

i am a holy place

Annabel Webster is a 21-year-old Southern Idaho gothic cowgirl, a cave dweller, made up of millions of dust particles glistening in the sun. She is inspired by crawl spaces, girlhood, and the middle of nowhere. Annabel attends Marymount Manhattan College in New York, but is haunted forever by the primordial vibrations of Idaho.

THE LADY WHO DARED TO GO APE

NANCY BREWKA-CLARK

Lillian Trimble Bradley (1875-1959), although given the honor of being called the first female director on Broadway, was also a prolific dramatist whose play "The Wonderful Thing" written with Forrest Halsey became the talk of the town in 1921. But what drove critics bananas that same year was her stage version of British author Edgar Rice Burroughs' "Tarzan of the Apes".

LILLIAN TRIMBLE BRADLEY:

Oh, heavens, don't get me started on critics. Ignorant, the lot of them. Of course, I shouldn't have expected such a motley assemblage of heavy drinkers and light-weight thinkers to appreciate the nuances of theater. After all, which of them could possibly have grasped the brilliance of Constantin Stanislavski's penetration of the human soul? I was so vastly fortunate to have studied with him at the Moscow Arts Theatre after my convent education in Paris. Oh, yes, for a small-town girl from Milton, Kentucky, I did get around. You see, my parents were peripatetic, always following the sunrise. From that poetic summation of their influence, I was happy to move on to marriage at the age of twenty-eight to dear, dear Bradley, who was sixty-five at the time. He went by the initials D.I., and do you know, I never did care what they stood for. He had his mysteries and I had mine. When he died, leaving me quite a bit of money and a simply fabulous estate, I created my own theatrical space and devoted it to the study of light and movement.

Thanks to dear, dear Constantin's insistence on all acting being a reflection of the innermost core of the actor, I insisted on the absorption of the character in a play into the soul of the artist portraying that character. And that is what led to my production at the Broadhurst Theater of *Tarzan of the Apes*.

Oh, even now I shudder at the stupidity of those who mocked it! I had deliberately embraced the challenge of taking Mr. Burroughs' tale of an English lord abandoned in the jungle as an infant and raised by simians to demonstrate the shining through of the human soul in the most primitive of conditions. But which of those critics grasped that point, or even glimpsed the poignancy of it? Inarticulate cries, they said, passing as dialogue! Oogh-oogh-oogh! Oh, beat those breasts devoid of human hearts, you fools, and do that jungle call incessantly, you witless parrots!

Ah. Well, I do get a bit roiled every time I think of the result of attempting to educate the great unwashed press. Their great joke was that the play ran on Broadway from September 1921 through September 1921. Those vile critics may have had great sport with me then, but I went on to make my mark for another two decades. Theater is hard work, every element of it. I would advise all women seeking to rise in this field to take a page from our elephantine kin and develop a thick, thick skin.

Nancy Brewka-Clark began her writing career at a daily newspaper chain on Boston's North Shore, where she interviewed theater legends such as Molly Picon, Douglas Fairbanks Jr. and Leonard Nimoy. Her plays and monologues have been published by Smith and Kraus, YouthPLAYS, and Routledge. Her NYC Playwrights' prize-winning 10-minute play High on Emma Safford can be viewed on YouTube as well as flash comedies for the long-running Brooklyn College series Gi60. Her short fiction, creative nonfiction and poetry also appear in numerous periodicals and anthologies.

YOU CAN'T DO ANYTHING WITHOUT ME

CHRISTINA HOAG

The bitch. The cold, evil bitch. After all I did for her, after all we went through, she left me? She thinks she's going to find someone better than me, that she's such a catch? She'll see. She's forty-five with a triple chin and Coke-bottle legs. She'll fucking see who she gets. I'll let her have her little life alone without me and she'll come running back just like she did when she first moved out five months ago. She called me up, crying hysterically from her car in some parking garage in Midtown. I took her back; I shouldn't have but I love her. I love her to death.

See, what Cath don't understand is I know her better than she knows herself. When I met her in Jersey two years ago, she came across so sweet and innocent, all loyalty and integrity. I fell for it. She had a great act going. She should've won an Academy Award. All she wanted was a way to get to New York and there I was.

I rescued her from that dump in Jersey, you know. She was in a small town way down the Garden State Parkway. I met her when I went down the Shore for a weekend. She was set up there with a nice house and a good job running a beauty salon and everything. I went into the salon for a haircut and stared at her the whole time in the mirror. She was so cute. Big eyes and a tiny, freckled nose. I asked her out. She said it would be a conflict of interest to go out with a client. I pushed. She acted kind of annoyed and said she had a boyfriend.

"Are you in love with him?" I asked. She didn't answer, just snipped. I knew I could reel her in.

I kept going down the Shore, dropping by the salon, bringing her flowers and chocolates. That always works with girls. I called her all the time when I went back to Manhattan. We talked for hours. She started telling me all her private stuff. I knew she liked me. I went down in the middle of the week once just to check up on her. You never know with women. They're sneaky, secretive. That was Cath all right, but I didn't find that out till later. Anyway, I waited around the corner from her salon and I saw this asshole pick her up. Well, she sure didn't go for looks, I'll say that much. Sure enough, two months later, she called. "Jimmy, you'll be very happy to hear this. I ended it with that guy." I was down the Shore that weekend.

From then on, every time I went back to New York, I was back down the Shore a couple days later. I couldn't stand not knowing where she was, who she was with. I was so in love with her. She cleared out a couple drawers for me in her dresser and stocked the fridge with stuff I like – purple Vitamin Water and chocolate protein shakes. I cleaned the bathroom for her, paid for a maid, just once though, she was fucking expensive. Cath bought me a real nice suit. When she moved out, I was going to rip it up, but I like it too much.

Cath blames me now for ruining her life? She wasn't doing shit in South Jersey. And she was a good hairdresser. She needed to get out of that dump and work at one of the salons on Fifth Avenue where she could make some real money. That's what I told her, anyway. See, I'll let you in on something. I wanted to get her away from all her friends. I had to get her to New York so I could have her to myself and she'd depend on me.

Lucky for me, Cath didn't have a lot of friends and she wasn't close to her family. She wasn't one of these girls always on the phone telling her mother or friends everything. I told her I liked her kind of being a loner, so she'd make more of an effort to be like that. Like I always told her that people were jealous of her, so she had to keep a distance from them. Like her nosy neighbor.

She also had a younger friend who was always dating and going out on the town. I told Cath she should have friends more her own age. That girl was too young for her. "Hon, you got so much more going for you than all these people," I'd say. "I'm the only one who sees your true worth." She'd laugh it off, but I could tell it soaked in. I'm pretty good at figuring people out.

I knew I could convince her to move to New York if I pushed hard enough. Most people are afraid to push for what they want. I'm not. I laid it on one night when we were walking along the Boardwalk in Atlantic City.

"Cath, you're forty-three. This is your last chance to make something of yourself. That salon is a shithole. You need to open your own salon in Manhattan. I can get you clients. I have a good real estate contact to find a locale. I'll remodel the place." I kept it up, too, kept hammering her. Like I said, some people you just have to push.

She didn't believe me until I took her to New York and showed her around and introduced her to my contacts. I knew a lot of people through my contracting business, although I haven't done too great for a couple years. I took her to fancy restaurants and clubs. I bought her clothes at Saks. She didn't want me to, but I insisted. I wanted to dress her up and take her out and show her off. She had a great body for a broad her age.

That's one thing I always liked about her. She never really realized what she had. I bought her a tan leather jacket that looks just like mine and a couple dresses, some short shorts. I never should've bought her clothes. She was probably going on dates in that form-fitting black dress I bought her. I should've taken a pair of scissors to that dress before she left, cut it up like I did with all her photos.

Cath wasn't like other girls I went out with. She was hard to impress. I had to really work at it, but I know how to turn on the charm. Hell, I'm a charming guy. I'm a good catch. I know I am. I took her for a special weekend to Southampton. I took another girlfriend there before Cath so I knew it would work.

I massaged her feet and made her a special bath with salts and everything. "I'm the only one to see the real you, the only one who really appreciates you and who you are, hon. Everyone else passes you by, but I see you for you."

"No one has ever made me feel like this, Jimmy," she said. "I think you were sent to me from heaven. You're my reward for doing the right thing my whole life." I practically melted when she said that.

"I want to marry you," I said. "I want to have a baby with you."

I know I have a problem with truthfulness, but this really was true. Cath really was my dream girl. If I married her and got her pregnant, she'd never run away from me. That's what's happened to me my whole life. People saw the real me and ran away. But Cath was different, or so I thought. Now I see how she sucked me in big time. She brought me coffee and an English muffin in bed every morning. If I told her I wanted more butter, she'd make it with more butter, crispier, she'd make it crispier. She even cut my toenails. She was really into doing that.

I love those crazy little quirks of hers. Sometimes I'd make her do stuff for me just to test how far she'd go. She came home from work one day to help me look for my keys. I'm always losing stuff. She brought gas to me when I ran out on the highway. She drove me twenty-five miles to the hospital when I had to have tests, went back to work, and then drove back to get me. No one took care of me like that, except my mother. She even has red hair like Ma. Cath is very kind, she really is.

I wish we could go back to that time, to the beginning. Why can't it be like that again?

You know, that fucking bitch left me without a dime in my pocket. Man, she's the cheapest broad I ever met. She uses coupons and buys gas at the Thrifty gas station. She has all this money in the bank from the sale of her house. The last time I checked her statement, it was more than $300,000. She's selfish and ungrateful, just like all the rest. I admit I lost my temper a couple times about her being a tightwad, but it worked. She started paying for more stuff to prove to me she wasn't cheap, that she wasn't just like all the rest. Like I told you, I know people.

But I'm getting sidetracked. Where was I? Yeah, so I got her to quit her job and sell her house and move to Manhattan. She wanted to just take some time off work and just rent out her house, but I talked her out of that. Pretty amazing, huh? I mean my dick ain't that big. She went and told my buddy George I manipulated her. She's nothing but a fucking con artist herself.

Cath was shy, hardly said a word around other people. It was better that way because she would say the wrong thing unless I told her exactly what to say. I mean I was so happy I had a girlfriend I took her around to meet all my connections and introduced her as my fiancée so they'd know she was a real girlfriend, not some bimbo. We dropped in once on Sheldon Squirel. I retiled his bathroom. He's a has-been, but he still acts, reality shows and stuff. He asked her where she lived. She said, "The Village." I couldn't believe it. When we got back in the car, I yelled at her.

"You should've said 'with Jimmy, in the Village with Jimmy'. Now he's going to think we're not really together. You don't realize that people are jealous, Cath. You just don't have the life experience I have. People are always going to try to drive a wedge between a couple, so they look for any kind of hole."

She started crying. That always made me feel bad, so I softened up. "We have to present a united front at all times, Cath. It's for our own good. I got ten years on you. You don't know people like I do."

I know I get mad. I can't help it. But she really knew how to push my buttons. She was always too nice to men. I don't mean the things I say when I'm mad. I mean, the names I called her, it was just because I was mad. That's all. She knows that. I feel so much better after I get mad. Like I need to get something out. But Cath made a big deal out of it. She was always a dramatic Annie, always exaggerating things.

Like when I grabbed her wrist and she fell against the bed. It was nothing, just a small push. So what? She made out like I threw her. She didn't even get hurt. I was upset because she was packing her bags to leave me. That was soon after I brought her to New York. I would never hit a girl. My father taught me to respect women. I blocked the front door and grabbed her shoulders.

"Do you want to throw away everything we have together?" I hugged her. "I love you. It won't happen again. I promise." She dropped her bags and hugged me back.

Another time she says I kicked the door in and smashed a lamp. I don't remember doing that. She almost called some domestic violence hotline on me. Can you believe that shit? That would've ruined my reputation. Good thing I got friends in the police department. I made sure she knew that, too. She should've understood. She knows I have low self-esteem.

Yeah, I know I'm fucked up. Who isn't? Cath? She's unsteady, passive-aggressive shit from growing up with an alcoholic father. She just puts on a good front. I told her things I never told anyone before, you know, shit about my childhood. My father used to smack me around, take me out back, and lay into me because he felt like it.

Then he'd take me to the emergency room when I couldn't see good or got a headache that wouldn't quit. I lied to the nuns at school about how I got the bruises. Told them I fell. I guess he got a little carried away, but them were different days. Everybody hit their kids back then. I woulda been a delinquent if he didn't slap me around.

I never told anyone that shit, except Cath. I went deep with her. She was very caring. She knows a lot about me, too much. But I know a lot about her, too. I made sure I got all her secrets out of her right upfront. Like her abortion, her affair with a married man. Secrets are good weapons in fights. I used them against her but so what. Cath knew they were just words. She knew how I was. I always made it up to her. I apologized. I promised to see a shrink.

"I can't live without you, Cath," I told her. "You're the best thing that ever happened to me." That's true, it really is. I had a real home with her. I felt like one of the guys, you know, with their wives always calling, nagging when they were coming home for dinner. I miss her. I miss her a lot.

When she moved out, she hid in a hotel. She did that just to make me come after her. She liked drama. I went from hotel to hotel looking for her. She accused me of stalking her. Can you believe that? It was romantic, that's what it was. Then she got her own place and a job, and we got back together again.

She needed me like I needed her. We were meant for each other. I know I made mistakes. She knew I wasn't good at relationships. Then five months later, she broke up with me just when I was going to take her on a trip to the Bahamas. I had it all planned out, and I was paying for everything to make up to her for the Hawaii trip. We went to Hawaii and well, I made her use her airline miles and pay for stuff. She was too nice to this friend of mine and I got jealous. We had a big fight. So, I was making it up to her. Yeah, I still had to put a few things on her credit card, but I was going to pay her back.

Then all of a sudden, she didn't want to go. She had no thought for the effort I put into planning for that trip. All the selfish bitch ever thought about was herself. "Jimmy, I told you I only wanted to go for five days, but you went ahead and booked it for ten. It's always all about you." That's what she told me. But she didn't want to go at all.

She goes, "You'll go into a rage. You'll get jealous because I'll talk to the waiter or something and you'll start raging. You're not safe to be with."

"So?" I says. "You can get on a plane and go home early."

She goes, "So I have to have my vacation ruined at any time because of your rages." Then she launched her grenade. "You know something, Jimmy. You're never going to change. This is it, end of the road. I don't want to do this anymore." The bitch got in her car and drove off. She left me standing there in the middle of the street. And I knew she wasn't going to come back to me this time. I knew it.

I tried to get her to see me, for coffee, anything, just as friends. I knew if I got her in front of me, I'd get her. She wouldn't be able to resist.

But she wouldn't do it. She changed her phone number. Bitch. She thinks she can just push me away like that. Fucking asshole.

She really changed. That wasn't the girl I fell in love with. Maybe it was her new friends at work, the shrink she'd been seeing. People were putting things into her head. She must've had someone waiting in the wings already. Her boss. I saw him looking at her.

So, go ahead, Cath, go right ahead. You'll never meet anyone like me again. You think you can make it on your own? You'll see. You'll fucking see. You can't do anything without me.

Christina Hoag is the author of novels "Girl on the Brink" and "Skin of Tattoos." She has had short stories, creative nonfiction essays and poems published in literary journals including Shooter (UK), San Antonio Review, Round Table Literary Journal and Lunch Ticket. In 2020 she won Honorable Mentions for essay and short story in the International Human Rights Arts Festival's Literary Justice contest and for essay and novel excerpt in the Soul-Making Keats Writing Competition. A former journalist, she reported from 14 countries in Latin America for Time, Business Week, Financial Times, The New York Times, Sunday Times of London, the Miami Herald and the Houston Chronicle. www.christinahoag.com.

PAPER BIRD

FROM THE SCREENPLAY "IMPOSTER"

SHEVAUN CAVANAUGH KASTL

KIMBERLY REYNOLDS, mid-'30s, is every bit the wilted flower, seated, languidly, on the floor, one strap of her flimsy silk camisole fallen from her shoulder. Her eyes are hazy, speech childlike with a puzzling laugh and erratic moods resulting from the benzo/opiate cocktail coursing through her system, a lifetime of damage, and a fractured sense of self. An unseen MAN, obscured by the camera is filming her.

KIMBERLY REYNOLDS

Sometimes I think I'm not real...

(*She ponders for a moment, then emits a peal of laughter.*) What a silly think to say! But people expect things, you know? Everybody wants a piece of you. (*She sighs, then absentmindedly begins picking at a tear in the wallpaper.*) So they take a piece and then they take another piece and another and suddenly it's like... Where'd I go? I'm only barely there, like paper. That see-through paper... What's that called? (*No response from the Man behind the camera, but she isn't really listening*) Translucent! *Translucent.* I like that word. (*Resumes picking at the tear*) So yeah it's like that. And I might just blow away with the wind.

(*Matter-of-fact.*) I think I'm mostly miserable. (*More giggles.*) It's just that darn wind keeps coming and WOOSH, sweeps me up, and I'm back in free-fall. (*Beat, then softly.*) But sometimes, I can fold myself up like origami. And the wind comes and I'm not falling. I'm *flying*... like a paper bird. That's when I'm closest to being happy. (*Off the Unseen expression of the Camera Man's face*) What, you think that's sad? Do I look sad to you?

There is hostility in her tone, but it only lasts a moment before being swallowed by yet another puzzling laugh. Kim collapses on the bed, lost in thought and somber.

Maybe I am sad. (*Beat*) But I don't cry. Not the way most people do, anyway.

(*Softly, under her breath.*) 'It's a mysterious place, the land of tears.'

The Camera Man moves closer. Kim's head flips sideways, averting the Camera's all-seeing eye, but catches a glimpse of herself in the mirror on the wall. Suddenly self-conscious, she bolts from the bed.

Turn it off. I don't want to do this anymore. (*Again the Man keeps silent.*) I don't want you taking my picture! Do you understand? (*Suddenly exhausted, Kim sinks down to the floor, cradling her knees, lost in thought.*) A photo lasts forever. It will still be here when I'm not. That makes me more than sad. That makes me irrelevant.

Shevaun Cavanaugh Kastl is a natural-born Storyteller. While she began as a Singer and Dancer in such professional NY stage productions as On the Town, Disney's Beauty and the Beast, and West Side Story, Shevaun later discovered her true passion - Writing and Filmmaking. Her first Short film, Conversations With Lucifer was honored among hundreds as one of four films to screen at the historic Grauman's Egyptian Theatre. Her second script, The Mourning Hour, won the title of Best Screenplay at the Slugline International Short Screenplay Competition and the film went on to receive critical acclaim with top honors at The Grand Off Film Festival in Warsaw, Poland, among many other festivals.

While Shevaun continues to write for the Big Screen, she has expanded her literary portfolio to include Poetic Prose, Short Stories, Monologues and One-Act Plays. Over the past three months, two of Shevaun's Stories "Somebody's Unicorn" and "An Act of Senselessness" were published in The Red Penguin Collection Anthologies - "A Heart Full of Love" and "The Roaring 20's - A Decade of Short Stories". Furthermore, Kastl's original Poem "Where I Find You," dedicated to the memory of her late father, will be published in the upcoming edition of Bloom, the Literary Magazine. She has now written three Feature Screenplays and is currently writing a Psychological Thriller as well as a Fantasy Novel.

THE NON-DATE

FROM THE SCREENPLAY "RESURRECTING RAPUNZEL"

SHEVAUN CAVANAUGH KASTL

(Christa arrives home from her date with Freddie completely besotted and starry-eyed. Her roommate, Jaz, has waited up, eager to hear every detail of Christa's EPIC night as she dines on a pint of Ben & Jerry's 'Chunky Monkey' Ice Cream.)

CHRISTA

Well, there was the standard first date stuff... We went to this cozy Italian bistro that he loves and it was candlelit and had those checkered table cloths and- Oh my God he speaks *Italian*! I mean he's not fluent or anything, but like, all during dinner he kept making these little statements to our waiter in Italian. *Which* he says is the most beautiful of the romance languages. (*Bobs excitedly on the couch.*) So anyway, I order the Chicken Francese and he orders the Chicken Parmesan... this is the best part. As soon as Romano- that's our waiter, *Romano!* drops our entrees, he immediately cuts off a piece of his Chicken Parmesan... and he puts it on my *plate*! So I, of course, cut off a piece of my Chicken Francese and put it on *his* plate. Isn't that just adorable? It's like the most couple-ish thing you can possibly do! (*Giddy squeals from both girls now.*) But wait! It gets better! At the end of the night, he walks me to my car and... (*relishing the memory.*) he gives me... a hug.

(*Jaz's enthusiasm immediately wanes and she stares incredulously at Christa.*)

Hey! Don't make that face! (*Slightly annoyed but eager to continue.*) Come on, listen!

As we backed away from... *the embrace*, there was this... moment. It felt like I was being pulled toward him. The physical chemistry was that intense, magnetic even. But at the same time, there was this realization that this could be it. I mean, (*Tearing up.*) this could be *love*. We could have a real future together and, strong as our physical desires might be, the hell if we're gonna potentially ruin what could be an adult, long-lasting relationship by moving too quickly, ya know? So it was like this battle going on inside, between our hearts and our wills. (*Beat.*) He kissed me on the cheek and then... he walked away. (*Soft, dreamy sigh.*) It was deep.

(*Several minutes later...*

After scrolling through Freddie's Facebook page, drooling over shirtless pictures, and gushing over candids with his dog, Michelangelo, the girls make a surprising discovery.)

He's GAY??? (*Reads the page.*) 'Sexual Preference – Interested in Men.' (*Beat.*) What?!?

(*Then, with a laugh that reeks of denial.*) Oh! That's a joke. Oh God, lots of guys, ALL these guys I know, they do that. They - they, they put down on their profile that they're gay and they're really not because it's funny. It's sooo funny and - is that the New York Fire Department shirtless on his layout?

. . .

(Shell-shocked and still in denial, Christa paces the room, trying to make sense of it all.)

No! No, no. This isn't - He's not - He's, he's... butch! A Real Man's Man, ya know? And he boxes. He's a boxer! And he *loves* rock music! His cell phone ringer is a Maroon 5 song! Oh my God, he's gay. (*In disbelief.*) He's gay. I just had a date with... a gay Man?

(As the realization sinks in, so do the beginnings of a panic attack. Christa starts to hyperventilate and rummages around the apartment, frantically, opening cupboards and drawers and closing them again.)

Romance languages? Oh my God! Oh - *Oh my God*. Even his fucking dog is named after an Italian painter! (*to Jaz.*) Where the fuck are the tissues? I'm talking about intense physical attraction and- and, and moments and he's probably sucking face with Romano as we speak!

(By this time, Christa has found a roll of Paper Towels, which she is using as tissues.)

Oh my God, I am such an idiot! (*Beat.*) I'm never getting married!!!

(In a fit of sobs, a crestfallen Christa departs for her room, but not before snatching the half-empty pint of 'Chunky Monkey' from the living room table.)

Before Shevaun Cavanaugh Kastl was writing films, she was performing on the stage. Her roots in theatre, performing in such professional NY stage productions as On the Town, Disney's Beauty and the Beast, Cinderella and West Side

Story, will forever be a piece of her and a crucial part of her journey as an actress and writer. Shevaun has become known for her fusion writing style of stage and screen and is simply thrilled to have authored two monologues from original screenplays. Scripts that drew heavily on her theatrical upbringing.

As a filmmaker and screenwriter, Kastl has earned acclaim. Her first Short film, Conversations With Lucifer was honored at the historic Grauman's Egyptian Theatre for its theme of recovery and addiction awareness. Her second script, The Mourning Hour, won the title of Best Screenplay at the Slugline International Short Screenplay Competition and the film went on to receive critical acclaim with top honors and nominations for Best Film, Best Cinematography, Best Editing, Best Direction and Best Actress.

While Shevaun continues to write for the Big Screen, she has expanded her literary portfolio to include Poetic Prose, Short Stories, Monologues and One-Act Plays. She also continues to act and you can catch her on TV in Criminal Minds, Revenge and Heroes.

THE PERFECT PURPLE CAPE

GAVIN DUERING

WILLEM JENSON, THE FIFTH:

(*Willem walks onto the stage wearing a funny-looking hat and a purple cape. He investigates the audience.*) Hello, my dear... (*Thinks.*) spectators and possible customers. I am Willem Jenson, *the Fifth*. Today I am selling a once-in-a-lifetime opportunity. What is this once-in-a-lifetime opportunity that you speak of, the most amazing Willem Jenson, *the Fifth*? Well, I am glad you asked, for today and today only will I be selling this Practically Perfect, Prestigious, Palatable, Perfect Purple Cape. Now I know you must be thinking: "this is a waste of my time." But, my dears, you couldn't be more wrong. Let me, Willem Jenson, *the Fifth*, tell you all about this beautiful Perfect Purple Cape. It is fireproof; I could set it on fire right now and be completely untouched – Nay! Unscathed. It is made of fine Indian silk and a lovely purple, so you could wear it on a nice stroll through Hyde Park. You also will be the talk of the *Ton*. Even the great Beau Brummel wears this very cape. That is not everything that this Perfect Purple Cape has to offer. It also has a hidden dueling sword compartment. It is on both sides for those that are of the left had variety. (*He begins to act out what he is saying.*) Now, let us say that you are indeed on a lovely stroll through Hyde Park. You are walking when, out of nowhere, these riff rafts jump out at you and... (*He looks around to see all the ladies.*) Ladies, I ask of you to please cover your ears, for what I am about to say is not suited for the faint of heart. I wish not to scandalize you and your fine sensibilities. (*Dramatic pause.*) You're surrounded by the ruffians and thugs. They think that you are completely defenseless, but you are wearing my fine Practically Perfect, Prestigious, Palatable, Perfect Purple Cape. You draw your sword, they scream, then you draw one of the four pistols, for dueling of course. You quickly dispatch of the ruffians and then you can continue your fine stroll with not a trace of blood. I will start selling them at, say, one thousand pounds. Who will buy first?

> Gavin lives in the mountains on the other side of the lake, where the eagle sowers and the thunder strikes. He is proficient in Ghukliak and belives that Bananans are a fashionable head covering.

MECONIUM ASPIRATIONS: A PLAY IN TEN BREATHS

MARK BLICKLEY

CHARACTER:

BABY---A plump infant dressed in diapers, attached to an IV drip.

BABY

I was born full of shit. It's called meconium aspiration. You see, I had what was the equivalent of a bowel movement when my mother went into labor because the umbilical cord was wrapped around my neck and that made me very, very nervous. This pre-natal stress caused me to fall victim to rapid heartbeats that threw me into rapid breathing.

Technically speaking, meconium isn't shit because I didn't eat any food, but it would be shit if it could be because it's the waste that collects around an embryo. When my heart started pounding and I begin gasping for breath, I accidentally swallowed this crap, so the moment I popped out of the birth canal, they slapped me into the Intensive Care Unit and pinched me full of antibiotics. I'm not certain why they did this to me because meconium, unlike true shit, is sterile and offers no risk of infection.

. . .

Yet here I lie, taped and punctured, in a no-frills basinet where I'm poked and prodded by masked intruders. It's not the most exciting of times, what with my unrequited cravings for the maternal tit, but it does give me time to think.

When you're born full of shit you can go one of two ways. You can either become a natural liar or turn into an inspired storyteller. I'll let you decide into which category I fit.

My mother is a very natural person. When her mucus plug came out —this block of black, bloody goop—and she knew my birth was imminent, she asked for the car keys from my father and drove to the woods surrounding a nearby park to squat and have gravity, not a team of doctors, assist in my birth. But the shithead found her and insisted on taking her to the hospital, where I now lie in a chilly room with a bunch of other tiny looking freaks who may or may not be swallowing their own shit.

I know, I know, you're thinking how the hell can a newborn be offering up journalistic observations, historical veracities, and judgmental insights? I can't answer that question, but I am leaning towards a belief in some sort of reincarnation. Maybe I'm the next Dali Lama.

Sometimes I feel like I have all the damn answers, but the truth is I don't even know what century this is or why the hell I'm being put here. I think I've been born into the past, but I'm not sure whose past, and that makes me kind of nervous. I get a feeling I might be here to hurt somebody. I wish you could tell me if I'm a boy or a girl because I'm not sure. I do know that I was spit out of warm slime and into a freezing room, and right away I learned my crying would get me what I wanted. Was that out of respect for who I'm going to be, or is it because they just see me as some sort of pathetic little bastard?

I can't seem to communicate with any of these obnoxious puffs of flesh in here, lying in their streaked stained diapers, sleeping and crying like a bunch of old fools. The grown-up sons of bitches in here gave me a spinal tap when I was less than an hour old. You believe that? Do they have any idea how painful that is? Sticking needles in you and draining stuff until your back feels like it's exploding? It still hurts. I'd like to shove a needle up their asses to see if I'd enjoy hearing them scream as much as they must've enjoyed hearing me.

It's hard to figure out whom to trust around here. I'm almost blind and naked and they won't let me have any secrets.

I think I'm going to need teeth to be able to tear into words, but right now I feel kind of sleepy. It's tiring trying to figure out if you're supposed to be an asshole or a genius. Why does the hatred of the world burn away at me while I sleep? All I can do is dream about being loved while drool drips down my chin. I shit my diaper and they rob me of my filth.

Do you want to adopt me?

Mark Blickley is a proud member of the Dramatists Guild and PEN American Center. He is the recipient of a MacArthur Foundation Scholarship Award for Drama. His latest book is the text-based art collaboration with fine arts photographer Amy Bassin, 'Dream Streams.' Blickley's art videos, 'Speaking in Bootongue', and 'Widow's Peek: The Kiss of Death' represented the United States in the 2020 year-long international world tour of 'Time Is Love: Universal Feelings: Myths & Conjunctions', organized by esteemed African curator, Kisito Assangni.

THE UNSAID OR THE SUPPRESSION

KERRI M. HOFFMAN

(*This is a climactic monologue, with the peak of emotional intensity occurring just prior to the end. The woman begins by expressing feelings of gratitude but then she speaks of painful emotions, until finally bitterness and then pity. As the piece begins, it appears as if she is speaking to her mother. The stage is dark and the audience does not see the woman speaking with anyone.*)

(*Softly*) Mom, I should have told you this sooner, but I feel that I have tried over the years. Let me start by saying that I think you were a terrific mother when I was growing up. I always felt secure, safe, and loved. I was a confident child with many friends. Looking back, I hold dear my memories of childhood, the teen years, and young adulthood. These were such precious, happy times for me. (*Pause*) Even though you were very sick when I was young and Grandma and Grandpa had to help Dad take care of me—I never felt deprived in any way. And I think that is truly a testament to you, Dad, and Grandma and Grandpa, working as a team to raise me. (*Pause*) The moral lessons you and Dad taught me have stayed with me throughout my life and now that I have a daughter of my own, I can honestly appreciate the values which you have instilled in me. You've taught me the importance of respecting others and treating people the way you would like to be treated. You always conducted yourself with class, treating all persons equally, from the sanitation worker who picked up our trash to the medical doctors who treated you over the years. (*Pause*) The importance of volunteering to help those in need is something that has made a lasting impression on me as well. I am an active volunteer for several organizations and charities. (*Pause*) But Mom, for the past few years I've felt that you and Dad have been a tremendous disappointment as grandparents. You never take the time to spend with me, even after I offer to pick you up to spend the day doing whatever you want to do. You and Dad have never once seen your granddaughter's numerous dance recitals. I have asked you both time and again to spend a weekend afternoon with us, to watch your granddaughter play in the park, compete in a soccer game and sing in the school chorus, only to be rebuffed with some lame excuse. (*Pause*) Your rejection makes me feel as though you and Dad think that you've done your job raising me and now you're finished. I can't figure out why you do not want a relationship with me as an adult or with your granddaughter. Sure, you *do* see us, but you only want to get together and when it is convenient for you. It baffles me, because when we speak on the telephone or get together for holidays, you seem to genuinely care about us. (*Pause with reflection*) I have come to the conclusion that you are just *so* incredibly selfish that you would rather miss a dance recital if it meant traveling into the angst-ridden city or you would rather miss a swim meet if it meant hitting rush hour traffic. I could go on and on... (*Pause*) It's sad because we *all* lose out in the end. (*Long pause with a sigh*) I'm done now. Part of my anger I *know* is my fault... because I wanted you to be more like me... (*Long pause*) As I walk away now, I'll try not to disturb the flowers on your grave.

(*She stands there a minute as the stage lights illuminate the headstone on her mother's grave, and then exits.*)

Kerri works as a writer/editor/blogger/attorney. She has written several plays which were produced Off-Off Broadway as semi-finalists in the New York City Strawberry One-Act

Festival and the Samuel French Playwriting Competition. Currently, her blog which focuses on essays, tips and recipes, for a healthy mind and body, can be found at www.mindbodyhealthytips.com. She has completed television writing courses at Columbia University and screenwriting courses at New York University. Kerri is currently working as a freelance copy editor /proofreader /press release Writer at Global Finance Magazine, an online international finance magazine.

YOUR CALL HAS BEEN FORWARDED.

SHELBI CORNELISON

Bryce (22) possesses an infatuating confidence. Upon first glance, it would not be out of the contrary for you to feel a displaced sense of "starstruck-ness." His aura produces the same familiarity of someone you've seen before, even if his name feels foreign on your tongue. His look, however, is distinct. A tattoo sleeve of artwork consumes his left hand and trails up his arm – becoming more simplistic the higher it reaches – until the images find a temporary resting place along the left side of his neck. His left arm is to the Sistine Chapel as his right arm is to a forgotten-about sketchbook, where only one small image is printed under his skin: the numeral "3" near the crease of his right elbow. He holds a phone in his right hand and puts it to his ear. He hovers over a table where a notepad, pen, and facemask reside.

BRYCE.

Hey...

        The name he wants to say, does not want to be spoken.

. . .

Anyway...I just wanted to...hah! Hi. Um...shit.

With his left hand, Bryce grabs the pen. He clicks it into use and proceeds to scribble a phrase onto the notepad.

Sorry. Why am I apologizing? H-how are you? How are you? Oh. Oh! Oh. I - I didn't know you were seeing someone. Her name - you said her name was - C-Carly? Carly! Me? No, no, no. I'm - I'm not seeing any- at least, not right now, anyway, you know how it is - catch feelings for someone in 5 minutes, lose them in 2 seconds. Call that the Bryce combo meal ah hah! No, I just actually wanted to call you to...um...

He writes down another note.

Haha! I wanted to let you know I'm releasing an album, *my* album...shit. Yeah, *My Album*, damn, wow that's crazy, I've never said that out loud before - sooo, you're the first one to hear me say that. Congratulations! But, I've had a lot of time to write since the world descended into fucking madness ah hah uh, and think? Think. A lot. Think a lot - I think a lot - I *thought* a lot, shit. There it is. Ahaha. I. Thought. A lot. About you. And mom and Ryland and Kels- Off topic. To the point. There's 13 songs and 3 of them are about you. And and and and I wasn't gonna release them but then I kept thinking and I thought and and I wonderered and I and after I recorded them I shredded the pages I physically shredded the pages and then then I I remembered that we haven't even talked haha like life stopped 6 months ago but we haven't even spoken in 9 and that is so...fucked up, bro, that is...so...

He clicks the pen open and closed, open and closed, open and closed.

A hundred and ninety thousand fucking people have died bro and every time my my phone has rung with a number I I I don't know there's there's a split second think thought that's it's gonna be about y-you and and and my mind fucking terrifies me because some- sometimes instead of a pit forming in in my stomach I'd smile. And that's so fucked up but I'd smile. And and I caught myself in the mirror doing it one day I was smiling and and and I - I've never seen the devil but I I think his eyes lo-look like mine. But then I I remembered that I have your eyes and they look *exactly* the same. And I'm in this paradigm because I want to hate you. I want to wanna hate you but to hate you I have to want - want to remember you and and I - I just want a fucking dad. That's all I ever wanted. And you took advantage of that. Yeah. I didn't think you'd say anything anyway. You can listen to the album, or don't. I don't really care. But it's out there. So just...wear a mask. I guess.

He pulls the phone away from his ear and sets it onto the table. He picks up the notepad and reads it. He writes a couple more phrases onto the paper. He picks the notepad back up. He reads it again. He picks his phone back up he taps on the screen. Suddenly, the dial tone can be heard. The call is on speaker. The phone rings and rings and rings. Until it stops. An automated voice takes over: "Your call has been forwarded to an automatic voice message system."

BLACKOUT.

Shelbi Cornelison, originally from Colorado Springs, Colorado, is currently a 3rd year undergrad in Marymount Manhattan College's Cinema, Television, & Emerging Media program with an unofficial concentration in Writing for the

Stage. On top of her artistic pursuits, Shelbi is a proud member of both Lambda Pi Eta and Alpha Chi Honors Societies. Post-grad, she aspires to pursue a career in screenwriting, with additional interest in both directing and performance. To keep up with Shelbi's upcoming and current creative adventures, follow her on Instagram @shelbicornelison and be sure to check out her digital portfolio.

KILLING TWO BIRDS WITH ONE STONE

SHELBI CORNELISON

SHARLOTTE

I don't really want to talk to you yet. To be blunt.

It's not that I don't have things to say to you. Because I have a lot of things I want to say to you.

I've rehearsed a lot of things I want to say to you, actually.

I just...

And I don't want to say I'm sorry because after the way we treated each other that would imply you have to say it too or that I'm expecting you to and I'm not I'm not I just I just want to know why we did it why we treated each other like y'know but I don't want you to answer that either so nothing I'm really saying makes any sense at all but I think that's because everything I'm thinking doesn't make any sense at all because I'm thinking that I think I know why people kill other people but like not like the premediated shit or at least I don't think so or maybe I do but I think I think I just mean I understand the impulse to crave it or at least crave the feeling of it when it's done and oh my God it just sounds like I confessed to murder and I swear to God I didn't but I think that sounds exactly like something someone who did commit a murder would say but at this point I think prison would probably be better than anything I'm going to say next so what the hell I killed someone not really well maybe I'll kill myself but haha that is not a funny joke I am sorry for that and um

A silence overtakes her trail of thought. She relishes in it for a moment.

I swear to God I wasn't lying about not wanting to talk to you. Well. I mean. I don't want to talk to you. But for some reason I need to. And I think I will always want to need to…talk to you…so…

Sharlotte finds the silence again.

Can we…I just wanna sit in this silence, for a minute, if that's okay? I mean I'm sure it's okay…given everything, I just mean it's still comforting with you. Silence is. Probably because even we can't figure out how to fuck up the purity of it yet. Which is astounding in itself, really. Sorry. Silence…

She takes another moment - out of pleasure. Discovering the irony through a laugh.

It kind of feels like time stops moving too, don't you think? It makes me feel like it's safe to pretend that our past isn't manipulating our future.

She takes another moment.

My sister posted a picture the other day. It was this spray-painted piece of driftwood she saw on the side of the road. I don't know if you saw it, I mean you liked it, but...I don't know if you read it. It just said, "We would've never known how to hate, if we first didn't understand what it means to love."

I was driving. She made me make a U-turn in the emergency lane - on the 405, mind you - just so she could take the picture.

She digests this.

It's kind of fucked up when you think about it. How one wouldn't exist without the concept of the other? Kind of like life and death. War and peace.

Another pause. She begins to understand this philosophy, in regard to the two of them.

Friends and...strangers.

She tries to find the comfort of the silence, but it has become lost. She can no longer hide in it.

. . .

Bryce told me when you asked him if he thought I was ever truly in love with you. I told him no. And I know he told you that I said that. So maybe this is his fault. Hah!

She finds herself in a small chuckle.

Sorry. Shit. I apologized and I said I wouldn't uh but...I guess Bryce just told you what I told him to. So I can't be mad at him just because I couldn't finish my sentence...apparently...so...

She makes sure they are still listening.

I didn't lie in case that's what you're thinking. Because I *was* never in love with you.

Her eyes move to anywhere but theirs.

Because I think we were a *bit more* than in love with each other. At least I was with you. And I think we still are. And I think we always will be...in love. Just...not in the way that we want to be. Yeah.

END.

Shelbi Cornelison is a current student in Marymount Manhattan College's Cinema, Television, & Emerging Media program with an unofficial concentration in Writing for the Stage. This piece, Killing Two Birds with One Stone, was the predecessor for a longer 10-minute scene entitled Backwards Into Each Other (which can be read/experienced on Shelbi's digital portfolio.) The voices featured within this monologue (as well as Your call has been forwarded. – also published within this anthology) exist in the same world. They are a sliver inside of a passion project Shelbi has been creating (on-and-off the page) since 2010. To keep up with this project – and other creative endeavors – follow Shelbi on Instagram @shelbicornelison.

A PEACH AND A TREE

LEE DANIEL

An oak tree, centerstage. It looks like any other oak tree, but there's something majestic about it because it is alone. Carrie approaches and sits.

CARRIE

Hi, um.

Hi. Hey.

...

I brought you a peach.

She produces a peach from her backpack or a pocket.

Your favorite. Our favorite.

She sets it down in front of the tree.

. . .

I mean, I know that like a bird or a squirrel is probably just going to eat it, but... It seemed right.

Like, flowers? But I didn't think you'd want flowers.

And you'd probably be happy to see the birds and the squirrels well fed. Um.

I don't really know how this is supposed to go. Or if you can hear me or if you're even here. It's...kind of presumptuous of me

to think you'd be spending the afterlife hanging around *our tree*, but when I visit... you. Um. Your... grave.

I don't really feel like you're actually *there*.

So I thought you might be here.

And if you are, then I'm really sorry it took me so long to visit.

It's hard. Coming back. I mean, I have come by but not like this. It hurt too much at first.

She waits for more words to come. Or maybe a response.

After you...

I kind of felt abandoned, honestly. Which I know is unfair. Obviously.

But I guess I just thought you'd always be around. That was the plan, you know?

...

I'm sorry if it seemed like I ever took you for granted.

And I guess I did. Take you for granted.

But I really loved you too, and I hope you knew that. Know that.

I still love you. A lot. And I hope you know that.

You always said you did, but I worry that you didn't really feel it.

> *A squirrel comes, snatches up the peach, and runs away.*
> *CARRIE laughs a little.*

There goes that, I guess. Sorry.

But I mean it's not like *you* were gonna it eat.

...

The tree looks taller.

Remember how it had stopped growing and we thought maybe it was sick? Well I think it must have started again after...I guess that's why I thought you might be here.

> *The wind blows.*

So hey I actually have something to tell you.

Um.

I'm moving. Soon.

For school. I'm moving to New York. Like we always said we both would. And I know you'd want me to, but...

I don't want it to be like I'm abandoning you or anything. Leaving you behind. I hope you wouldn't think that. That I'm going to forget about you or anything. I don't think you would, but I wish I could know for sure.

I wish you'd say something.

LEE DANIEL

> *She waits. For a while. Something changes in her.*

God, okay. I don't...I don't know what I'm doing.

I don't think you're here, and if you are, I don't think you want me here.

So I'm gonna...go. I'm sorry.

> *Carrie stands up and starts to leave.*
> *A peach falls from above and thwacks Carrie on the head.*

What—

> *10 or 20 or 30 or 100 more peaches rain down.*
> *Somehow, none of them are damaged. It's breathtaking.*

I—

Thanks.

> *End.*

Lee Harrison Daniel is a New York based playwright, producer, and occasional performer who writes queer magical realism and experimental plays that explore all the "in-betweens" of young adulthood. After growing up just outside of Detroit, MI, Lee moved to New York in 2017 to pursue a degree in playwriting and new media at Marymount

Manhattan College. Since then, their plays have been produced by Water House Collective and The Masked Collective, and they are currently a creative producer and resident artist at First Kiss Theatre Company.

ABOUT THE EDITOR

JK Larkin is a Long Island-based writer and recent graduate of Marymount Manhattan College. He is the two-time published author of "not kidding." and "Side Street". His body of work draws heavily upon themes of existentialism, morality, and the struggle to connect in a deeply divided world. Follow him at @jksnotkidding and @jklarkinart on Instagram, @jksnotkidding on TikTok, or @JKLarkinTM on Facebook to keep up to date with his artistic journey.

ALSO FROM THE RED PENGUIN COLLECTION

Realiteen: Reflections On Growing Up

What Lies Beyond: Sci-Fi Stories of the Future

A Trip For The Books

I Can't Find My Flashlight

The Moments

The Beauty Within—Stories of Spirituality, Faith and Love

'Tis The Season—Poems to Lift Your Holiday Spirits

We Made It!—Essays Reflecting On The New Year

Stand Out—The Best of The Red Penguin Collection, Vol. 1

It's The End Of The World As We Know It

A Heart Full of Love—A Collection of Romantic Short Stories

The Roaring '20s—A Decade of Stories

the flower shop on the corner

www.ingramcontent.com/pod-product-compliance
Lightning Source LLC
Chambersburg PA
CBHW030557080526
44585CB00012B/409